PIANO PLAYING

A Positive Approach

Richard Collins

UNIVERSITY
PRESS OF
AMERICA

LANHAM • NEW YORK • LONDON

Library of Congress Cataloging in Publication Data

Collins, Richard 1928-
    Piano playing.

    1. Piano—Instruction and study.   I. Title.
MT220.C75   1986   786.3   86-9078
ISBN 0-8191-5367-2 (alk. paper)
ISBN 0-8191-5368-0 (pbk. : alk. paper)

All University Press of America books are produced on acid-free
paper which exceeds the minimum standards set by the National
Historical Publications and Records Commission.

ACKNOWLEDGEMENTS

The author gratefully acknowledges the following for permission to quote copyrighted material:

G. Henle Verlag, for permission to reprint excerpts from the Chopin Nocturnes (Copyright 1966), Preludes (Copyright 1956), and Waltzes (Copyright 1963), and the Beethoven Sonatas, Vol. II (Copyright 1953).

New Directions, Inc., for permission to reprint excerpts from Siddharta, by Hermann Hesse (Copyright 1951).

CONTENTS

CHAPTER ONE

A POSITIVE APPROACH

Picture this. We've all seen it before. A rather thin young lady enters from the wings, slithers across the stage, appearing not at all to notice that the audience is there, much less acknowledge their applause with a bow, and quickly seats herself at the piano. With a kind of hopeless shrug, she throws herself into her performance. And what comes out? Sometimes broken patches, the excellent mixing at will with the incoherent. Or perhaps a flat, even-paced, rather dull, but accurate performance. Or worse yet, an entrance into the piece, which rather quickly crumbles, to be replaced by another entrance, which again crumbles, and again an entrance, and again, until in tears she rushes off, determined, with some justice, never to do that again.

Fortunately, this is not always the case. Quite often an inexperienced student will come up with quite a credible, even inspired, performance. But usually "nerves" take their toll on almost every attempt to present music publicly, and rarely is it that a student doesn't say afterwards, "If only I hadn't been so nervous! I really knew the piece much better than that!"

This nervousness is only a symptom of an even more serious condition among most young pianists. They lack conscious control over their playing. Most often when something goes wrong they are simply stuck and can't go on, and all their many hours of practicing doesn't seem to help them at all. So what is wrong with their practicing? And more than this, what is wrong with their attitude towards performance?

We all know the delights of an inspired performance, the magic which produces seemingly effortless, yet meaningful playing. We often say, "If only I could have that feeling all the time when I play, instead of just now and then."

What we need is a way of practicing, a way of thinking about music, which allows this divine inspiration to flow at will. The problem is, I think, that piano study has traditionally been the narrow pursuit of a goal: the "perfect" performance. The playing of every passage, every trill, every note, even, was

1

mastered technically or analysed intellectually. Instead, this book will attempt to show that there is another way, a more meaningful way, a more positive way, the way of being more receptive, which can lead to piano mastery. By "receptive" is meant being open at every moment of performance, and in every moment of practicing, to the inner guidance which is available to every person. Some call this guidance divine, and indeed it probably is, but it is located within us, and need not be sought outside. Reliance on this aspect of ourselves does not eliminate the need for practice nor the need for discipline. Far from it. It merely opens the doors within us to use a part of ourselves which is always ready and available. And when used it can make our practicing into a performance, our work into pleasure, and our every effort becomes imbued with creativity instead of drudgery.

Probably the first thing to realize is that we are not really conscious of all the thousands of impulses that go into producing a beautiful, inspired performance. In our best work we are supremely conscious of the _effect_ we are striving for at any given moment, but the particular _means_ to achieve this effect we most often leave to our unconscious. Just how far to move the wrist, just how much weight to give each note of a chord, just exactly the speed of that melodic ornament, the degree of rubato here or there, are left to our unconscious to give us. Our conscious mind is more concerned with the whole, with how the character and the energy of the sections we are creating will work in that whole and produce that whole. As we come down to the physical, or even the musical, details, when we are truly inspired, we let them happen as they will. Yet they "happen" with a kind of logic, certainty, and vitality unattainable with the closest analysis or with the utmost mental effort.

Is this a mystery? I don't think so. What is happening in these supreme moments is that a higher source takes over the actual running of the ship, as it were, and we are left free to plot the course and enjoy the ride. A neat trick, of course, but how do we practice so that we can predictably achieve this pinnacle of performance? What method can we use if all must be somehow so flexible in performance that it can obey the precise but changeable directions given by the inspiration of the moment? In short, how do we practice for an improvisation?

I think the answers in the past have not been satisfactory. Most teachers have emphasized a technical approach, an approach through the study of the physical mechanism, through the building up of learned patterns of finger movements. The idea was that since performance was a miracle, we couldn't really touch it, and therefore our efforts should be confined to the un-musical aspects of the piece. Then, during the performance, it was supposed that we would forget all the mechanical habits produced by such practice and be able to simply "let go" and produce an inspired performance. Well, surprisingly enough, this method did work now and then, but more usually the patterns of practicing persisted and the attempt at letting go produced very little in the way of beauty.

For some the opposite approach was used: decide everything in advance, and leave nothing to chance. The mind was turned loose on the score and the "correct" stylistic and pianistic solution to every phrase was carefully calculated. And, while a greater degree of consistency of effect was achieved with this method, the heights of beauty and the inspiration of the moment were most often lacking.

The solution, it seems to me, is to emphasize the improvisatory nature of the music from the beginning, so that whenever one experiences the piece, whether it is in the earliest period of one's study or during a performance, the conscious mind will always be concerned with conceptions of character and shape, and the fingers and arms will always be willingly, and usually unconsciously, working to manifest these conceptions. It means learning your music "by ear", so that the sound you produce on the piano always starts with a sound-image in your mind, and it is that sound-image alone which directs the fingers. The pathways established are from the hearing part of the mind, through the fingers, to the actual sounds produced, not the more usual pathways of one finger-movement connected to the next, and to the next, etc.

It is the purpose of this book to demonstrate how such an approach is possible to achieve, either in one's own performance or in the performance of one's students. The learning process will be explored in enough detail to enable the serious pianist to be his own teacher in applying these principles to his own playing. In essence we always teach ourselves, anyway. The best a good teacher can provide is some information, an encouraging environment, and an occasional example for inspiration. Very little can actually be taught. Rather, it is caught, as the receptiveness of the student responds to all the stimuli available, from all the music he hears, from all the theories he encounters, from all the advice his teachers and others give him, and most of all from the inner lessons he receives from his own experiences.

So, when the information available in this book reaches the student, if it seems right to him, and if he has the discipline to apply it consistently, perhaps he will incorporate this new approach into what he already has, and will find himself the better for it. We hope so.

CHAPTER TWO

LOOKING AT THINGS AS A WHOLE

How do we learn anything? We generally start out with something we would like to be able to do, but are unable to do. So we try one method to see if it will work, then we try another, and so on. With each attempt we find we have made some progress towards our goal, and eventually we do reach that goal. In this manner we are learning how to find our own way through the difficulties. We generally feel that what we have learned may work best for us, but that our solution may not necessarily fit as well into someone else's situation.

But still there are times when one feels one has learned something basic, something which can be shared with others. One feels that he has achieved some insight into the general problem of how to go about learning anything, and often he feels a desire to share this discovery.

Thus it has come about that today there are any number of popular books, mostly in the health fields, which emphasize the benefits of considering the human apparatus as a "holistic" entity. These many practitioners each feel they have found something of universal validity in their work. They argue that since every part of us affects every other, we should consider ourselves as one whole thing and start our thinking from there. In addition, psychological studies demonstrate that while the consideration of the parts will not necessary lead to an understanding of the whole, yet the contemplation of the whole must of necessity include all the parts that make up that whole.

But how does this thinking in terms of the whole affect activities which take place over a period of time? Ask anyone who cooks without a recipe. They will tell you that somehow it "just seemed necessary" to add so much of this or that ingredient. Their continued imagining of how the whole thing would eventually taste gave them the information as to what would be the necessary ingredients to produce that taste.

And so it is with public speaking. The politician who is attempting to influence an audience may

5

not know exactly how he will give his speech, but he will constantly be aware as he proceeds how his words are progressing towards his goal. He knows the effect he is trying to produce in his audience and he judges the response as he goes along, adjusting as necessary to produce the desired result.

The performance of piano music is in many ways similar to these two examples. It contains the element of improvisation, since, no matter how well prepared one may be, in a performance one must deal with the actual sound made in any moment of time, and one must connect these sounds one after the other to produce a meaningful whole. One's re-creation of a phrase, a melody, or a complete section will always vary somewhat from performance to performance. In fact, this is one of the elements in a performance which gives it vitality. The audience never quite knows what will happen because the performer never quite knows what will happen. He is concerned, like the politician or the cook, with the total effect his work will produce, and at every moment is concentrating his energies on each detail as it creates its contribution to that total effect.

In what terms does the pianist conceptualize his striving after effect? What does he think about? Shape, for one thing. Character, for another. These qualities are ever present in music and provide a continuously changing image for him to concentrate on. Other things, like texture and metrical pulse, are more generalized and less related to individual moments in time. But any characteristic which relates to how the time is directed and filled are the matrix which the mind fastens on as it produces the forward movement of the music.

And, since this is where our mind is when we are performing, it makes all kinds of good sense to develop a practice method which encourages our similar attention as we go through the learning of a piece. Our practicing ought to be as much like our performance as possible. But so often we say, "How can I work on the music until I've learned the notes?" The answer to that is to work on the music at the same time you are working on the notes. Not a very revolutionary idea, really, but not as easy to do as to profess to do. Almost immediately, when the slightest problem in learning arises, we collapse our attention from the musical to the digital, and thereby engage

6

significantly lower centers of thought. And are these higher centers ever re-engaged? Sometimes they are, sometimes not. Once the distraction has been made, there is a part of us that always thinks of this or that section in a physical, muscular, way and these thoughts do not contribute to the connecting of the small part with the whole. They don't answer the question of how this measure contributes its moment of time to the sequence of musical events. Instead, consideration of a passage as "difficult" serves to isolate it from the mainstream of the piece.

In general, I believe this concept of thinking of performance in terms of whole things can best be understood as a process of "making" rather than one of "doing". When one is mostly thinking of "getting it right" or "playing it perfectly", the result, when one is successful, is in terms of what one has "done". But when you are putting together a work of art in time, the thought at the end, when successful, is on what you have "made". And how much more prone to nervousness and worry is the person who is concerned with fulfilling the obligation or duty to achieve perfection! It can't be done! And the performer, underneath it all, knows this. He knows that "perfection" is a model, at best, and though it might be possible to play a piece without error, truthfully, would that make it "perfect"? It could not, because we define "perfect" as being the best performance possible, yet we know that it is _always_ possible to subtly change the shape of this or that in a piece, thus making another interpretation equally as "perfect" as the first. Hence, our concept of "perfect" does not work as an aid in learning to perform. Instead, it just makes us nervous that our human short-comings will somehow be exposed in the performance and all will be ruined.

Contrast this with the other approach. Should there be an error or a poorly executed phrase, the thoughts of the performer are constantly directed forward towards the salvaging of what is left of the piece. "More beauty is yet to come," he thinks, "and I must produce the best total effect possible." Hence, instead of breaking down because of a minor disaster, he quickly re-groups his forces to concentrate on the next moment, and the next, etc. And at the end he has, indeed, "made" something worthwhile.

The effect this approach has on one's playing, in

general, is that it makes performance more fun! It
takes the worry out.   It is also more positive, because it emphasizes what one is producing, not what
one is worried one won't produce.

CHAPTER THREE

LEARNING PIECES BY EAR

Granted that we would rather be concerned in our piano playing with "making" rather than "doing", with creating a work of art rather than meticulously obeying a set of directions, what is the best way to achieve that goal? What aspect of the mind can we use which is consistent with that goal?

What we need is an approach which will work equally well in the details as in the whole. It must be an aspect of mind equally at home in the highest concepts of artistic creation and in the lowest degrees of momentary thought. It turns out that our attitudes towards the sound of music itself exhibit this universality. The sound of music can be thought of as each tiny microsecond of time in all its various attributes: tone, volume, pitch, etc., and it can be thought of as the moments of time accumulate into larger units: texture, rhythm, phrase, etc. And this process of expansion in time can eventually include the whole of the sound, i.e., the whole piece itself.

The blessing of using sound as the organizing parameter is that the extra-musical effects of our playing attach thamselves without mental effort to this sound-image. The character of a phrase, section, or whatever, is most easily imagined as having a particular kind of sound. Words come to mind such as "heroic", "martial", "invigorating", or, at the other end, "subdued", "obscured", "distant". Every one of these hundreds upon hundreds of wonderfully descriptive characterizing words can be immediately connected in our minds with the specific qualities of the sound which will produce these effects. Thus, we have but to concentrate on the effect desired, and the sound in all its details, as well as in its totality, is immediately manifest. It doesn't always come out of the piano so easily, but having it in our minds is the first requirement for getting it to do so.

And now we come to the point where we are concerned with "how to do it"--how to actually go about learning a piece of piano music from this point of view. The most important thing, it seems to me, in the learning of anything is to be interested in learning it. And one thing that will certainly assure interest is if you love the piece. I remember the

9

great kindness of one of my teachers, who, instead of assigning me a piece, would give me four or five from which I could make my own selection. Considering the amount of time and effort involved in preparing a piece for performance, it seems only fair and sensible not to embark on such a project without love. Sometimes such a love must be cultivated, it is true. Unfamiliarity seems to be the thing that breeds contempt in music, not familiarity. A little forced exposure to a new style can lay the groundwork for an eventual deep appreciation of that style.

Another thing that one must have before he can properly begin is a score that clearly shows the composer's intentions. Since every mark a composer writes is there to give us information, we really have no business using scores which have been tampered with. The composer doesn't just write the notes, he writes the phrase marks, the accents, the staccatos, and adds every other detail of editing which he considers might contribute to a greater understanding and a more accurate translation of his music. So often a well-meaning editor will "equalize" parallel passages, when it might have very well been the composer's intent to keep such places distinctly different from each other.

There are cases, especially in earlier keyboard music, where the editor can provide great assistance to the uninitiated through the realization of ornaments, appoggiaturas, etc., and through the inclusion of footnotes in regard to the style of the period. As long as the editorial and original notations are graphically distinct this presents no problem. But when the performer is deprived of his right to be his own editor we are placed in the position of not knowing what the composer has said. How can we ever learn to "interpret" if we don't start with what is "given", i.e., the composer's original score?

Our first reading of a projected new work is often one of the most exciting experiences we will ever have with the work. Our enthusiasm is intense, as in this act of discovery we enter the world of the composer and his creation. So often we have the completed piece in our inner ear in all its glory, notwithstanding the mountains of wrong notes and rhythmic garblings our sight reading produces. This is an ideal state. All the presence of the music is there, without any worry as to technical completeness.

But for many of us, successive readings of the work become less and less spontaneous, as our minds succumb to the pressure of solving difficulties, making decisions, etc. Our hearts become subdued, and we forget the original impetus of love which the work generated at first contact.

One must approach each difficulty with the same love one has for the work as a whole. If you love the passage its "difficulty" becomes transformed into a search for the positive values of the section in question. Instead of asking, "How will I ever get to be able to play this part?", one asks, "How does this part contribute its own distinct character to the effect of the whole?" Instead of closing one's attention down to consider something as being isolated and mechanical, one asks for input from the music itself to give us better understanding of the nature of its essential characteristics, and in bringing these characteristics into existence as sound, we generally are able to "solve" the problem. We use all of ourselves in this positive approach, not just our mental or physical equipment. Because we look at it as a total situation we of necessity are involving our total selves in its solution. One might sum it up: think small, be small; think big, be big. If our attention can encompass all the elements of the music and its effect as sound, we are challenged to engage our entire selves--physical, emotional, mental, and spiritual--in the preparation of the piece for performance.

In order to play a piece "by ear" one must be able to hear each sound before it is produced. The mental image of each tone must precede the physical actualization of that sound, otherwise we are simply using our fingers and arms to organize the music. But somehow we must get the fingers and arms to play the keys or the music will not sound at all! Not many pianists can simply hear what they want and sit down the first time and realize these sounds in their completeness. Such talents exist widely in the popular and jazz fields, however. And, in fact, it is considered pointless to aspire to any kind of success in these fields without this ability.

But in classical music we must reproduce what another person has conceived, and this re-creative act is substantially different from the improvisational act of the popular keyboardist. The tendency in clas-

11

sical music is to give up the creativity of the improvisational process in favor of the highly organized, totally controlled performance. Thus, letting the music flow from one sound to the next, from one intense moment to the next, seems less important than getting it right and eliminating mistakes.

In order to form a basis from which to fight this over-organized mental approach, we must strive from the beginning to work on learning the inner sounds of a piece at the same time we are working on the motor movements necessary to create the physical sounds. There are as many ways to do this as there are people doing it, but certain categories do come to mind.

Some music is simple and straightforward enough to be learned directly as sound. We simply let our hands proceed from sound to sound, and the unconscious learning processes work the details out on their own, and, lo and behold, we find one bright day that the music is playable in its entirety without the score and without error.

But, obviously, this is seldom the case, and with most beginners this is almost never the case. Some intermediary method must be used. Many find that considering which finger to place on which key is a fail-safe method. They train the fingers and the music emerges. Those who use this approach will need to consciously hear in their minds every note, singing each sound as the fingers produce it. This means they must play the hands separately if they sing out loud, but fortunately this imaging can also be done silently instead of out loud, and both hands will then be able to play together. The secret is to play at a slow enough tempo so that there is no doubt that every single note is first imagined, then played. The surprising benefit is that this very slow practice need only be done once or twice, speeding up considerably thereafter, quite unlike slow physical or mechanical practice, which must be repeated many times for it to be effective. What one is training is the mind, not the muscles. The muscles will obey the mind, so it is the mind we must work with. I don't think anyone wants to let the muscles train the mind. Although, I know, we have all heard performances in which this process has occurred, and the musicality of the performer in such cases seems deeply obscured. The performer himself is usually at a loss as to how to

retrieve such a performance and is not able easily to
change it for the better. Instead, a re-learning
through slow practice must occur, in which the ear is
trained to take command.

Part of the learning process also seems to
involve watching our hands at work, and organizing the
sequence of notes by where they occur on the keyboard.
We think, "First this one here, then that one there,
then these keys get struck, etc., etc." For many this
procedure is the central focus of attention in the
beginning of their study and memorization of a piece.
Certainly in complex or dissonant contemporary works
it is probably the most commonly used method. I can
personally attest that although I performed the Ives
First Sonata about forty times in public, it wasn't
until the last dozen or so times that I could honestly
say I was able to hear every sound in my mind before I
played it. The "geographical" approach gave me the
security I needed, and it was only after repeated
performances that this thorny piece was finally tamed
and properly learned by ear. The method used in the
interim was that of knowing where to put my hands and
imagining the quality of the sound, even though the
image of the actual pitches didn't completely enter
the picture until later. Most contemporary music
has to be learned this way. It certainly is a lot
quicker, but also caution must be exercised because it
is less reliable than the "by ear" method. If more
than a day or two goes by without work on our piece,
we find we must go back and review heavily what we had
accomplished earlier.

Still, for many, this approach is the most useful
in getting pieces learned quickly, whether in contemporary or in traditional literature. Each person has
already organized for himself the surest, easiest,
most natural pathways of learning, and should this
"geographical" approach suit you best, you will choose
it, consciously or not. The same principle applies
here as before. In order to ensure that the ear is
learning the music and that it can control the playing
and not just follow what the hands have learned, slow
practice must be pursued until the image of the sound
of each note precedes the formation of each physical
sound. Then the pathway will be formed, quite automatically, from the sound-image to the hand movement,
as surely as Pavlov's dog responded to the bell by an
increase in the flow of his salivary glands. Fortunately, the automatic responses of the body are just

13

that: automatic. We must learn to work with this knowledge and turn it to our advantage. The blessing is that we are controlling this unconscious process by a conscious mechanism. Our ear, and the brain power associated with it, is constantly under our conscious control. We can think of any combination of qualities associated with sound that we want, and then let the body unconsciously obey the order to produce these sounds. Most of the time our only limit is our imagination.

The important thing to realize is that just playing slowly won't work by itself. We must be extremely alert, and stoically disciplined, to resist allowing ourselves to simply "play" the piece, once the physical mechanism is secure. The temptation, especially if aided by long training in physical success, will be to consider that we are "in control" as soon as we can play the piece. Not so, because the part of us we want to control the playing, the conscious mind, cannot operate through the closed pathways of muscular learning. So we must be ever vigilant that in our practicing we are truthfully attempting to get the ear to learn the piece, as well as the hands. The joys of control are the rewards. You are less nervous if you know you are in control of your performance. You begin to trust the pathways of the mind that produce exactly the right sound for you, even though you never told yourself "how", but just told yourself "what". This confidence does take time and many learning experiences to be produced, but when it comes, one's attitude towards performance undergoes a profound and drastic change.

Other methods of learning involve, for some, memorizing what the page looks like. A few people are blessed with this visual gift to a high degree; others, it seems, not at all. Also, some memorize by analysing the music harmonically or structurally, and find this aids their security in performance. As long as the music is heard before it is played, eventually these other methods will fall into second place behind ear-memory. After all, if we were not ear-oriented we wouldn't be pianist-performers. For those who are not ear-oriented, but still wish to learn how to play the piano, one or another of these other methods will naturally have to predominate, and all that I have said about learning by ear will not have much meaning. But, even so, I have been surprised many times in my teaching to find that the "un-musical" student through

14

great determination and self-discipline can find musical pathways towards control of the performance which I have been unaware of. When I see this happen, I know I don't have all the answers. Motivation is still the number one learning device, talent or no talent.

Once again I should emphasize that just pounding it out slowly is not the solution. What you are attempting to produce is a duet between the sound in your mind and the sound in the strings of the piano. It can help to open the piano up, so you will hear more of its sound. And also you might experiment with playing pianissimo, so that the sounds in your mind can seem to dominate the tones you actually produce. You must always play with some specific effect in mind, with the characteristics of tone, shape, and texture clearly pictured. Observe every mark on the page. It's true you can "add them later", but why learn one thing and then have to un-learn that as you try to learn the second way later on? As soon as you can play the piece without the music you are in danger of by-passing all the remainder of the notational assistance the composer has provided. We tend to think of the piece then as belonging to us, and I know from my own experience that it is very tempting to practice from that point on without consulting the score. Danger! Instead, once or twice a day a run-through with the eye at work to see every phrase and every accent and every other bit of minutiae in the score will help bring your performance closer to the composer's desires.

Sometimes it is not necessary that the entire piece be practiced slowly. All one must do in that case is to slow down at those corners or complex regions where the ear would tend to lag behind. A little experience with this method will give you the ability to know where to slow down. In addition, a long series of staccato sounds may need to be played legato a couple of times. These slow "ear-training" sessions will usually bring any recalcitrant sections up to the performance level of the rest of the piece quite quickly.

Complex sounds can often be more easily grasped by the mind if they are heard from the bottom up. I presume this has to do with the physics of the overtones, but I don't really know. I can only say that it works. One would think that the top voice could dominate more easily than the bottom, because one could hear the top and include with it the harmony underneath, and in traditionally harmonized music this is generally true. But I am speaking here of that other type of music--Schoenberg, Ives, Berg, etc., in which the density of the vertical texture must be absorbed by the ear in any way one can. Try thinking from the bass line as an aid to imaging the sound. It may work for you.

In highly expressive music the shape of the phrase may be the easiest way to group together thickly written sounds. It provides a link between individual moments when there is no real melody or bass line to start with. Remember that it is not just the geometrical shape, but it is that plus the vocal, or rather the expressionistic, shape to which I refer. Decide where the climax is and hear in your mind as soon as you can, even without actual pitches, what the conductor would ask for if this were to be an orchestral piece. Pianistic color should very easily come to mind at this point. Every feature of the music which gives it a more specific identity in your imagination will make it more meaningful and thus easier to remember and produce. And, as noted before, the earlier in your practice this occurs, the less adding-on and re-learning you will have to do later.

It is important to remember in all this that learning piano music for performance can be a conscious process. And this conscious control can continue throughout one's practice right into the performance phase. The wonderful thing is that one can use the instantly creative technique of improvisation in the performance of previously composed music. As long as one has control of the forming essence of the music in one's mind, through ear-imagination, that conscious control is never let go. The more detailed the mental picture one has, and the more refined the character of the aural image, the more the conscious mind is sure to be used. What gives the performance vitality, however, goes beyond mind. It is in the singing impulse, that undefinable urge to produce beautiful music. By keeping our attention from the very beginning on this creative flow through the learning of our pieces by ear, we exercise and stimulate this central singing core in each of us.

16

CHAPTER FOUR

TECHNIQUE, OR HOW TO DO IT

By "technique" is meant the ability to play a piece of music. Nothing more nor less. For a brick-layer, technique is the ability to make a wall that looks right and is structurally sound. For a baker, technique is the ability to consistently produce excellent bread and pastry. So for a pianist, technique is the ability to consistently produce beautiful piano music.

Most of our technical ability is unconsciously acquired. We want a certain effect, and the body acts as a whole to produce that effect, correcting itself until the effect is achieved. At the basic level, consider how we learned to drive a car. At first our movements of the steering wheel were inefficient and clumsy, but as we saw the effect our movements had on the path of the car we adjusted them. Now the mere thought of where we want the car to go triggers the exactly appropriate arm movement to get it there.

Think of the baseball player. He uses his "natural coordination" to achieve the results he wants. When he sees the shortstop move to cover the runner stealing second, he doesn't think, "Lower the left wrist, keep the weight on the right foot an instant longer." Instead he thinks, "Hit it where the short-stop was!" The individual muscle movements work as a concerted whole, unconsciously coordinating to produce the effect. And his conscious mind is only concerned with the effect.

Think of the waiter carrying a trayful of drinks. If he should trip, his one and only thought is: "Don't spill the drinks!" All kinds of muscular movements may be called into play to obey that command.

Think of the last time you almost bumped into somebody as you rounded a corner to find them directly in your path. Gymnastics worthy of an Olympic competitor can take place at moments like these, completely spontaneous and completely unconscious.

My point in bringing up all these examples is to remind us that the body acts as a whole with superb efficiency, coordinating highly complex movements with a single conscious thought. We sometimes forget in

our zeal to train and strengthen various parts of ourselves, that while it is necessary for a muscle to be
strong and agile, it is not necessarily required that
it learn to act independently of the rest of our body.
Independent action of a part may be required to build
up muscle tone and responsiveness, but a muscle is
more useful to us if it is allowed to act in coordination with other muscles. And natural, spontaneously
generated coordination is much more efficient and
responsive to command than is mechanically oriented
movement.

Hence, when one encounters what one might consider to be a difficult passage, it is far more
advantageous to approach it from a viewpoint which
will allow our natural coordinative ability to operate, than it might be to consider what the hand or
fingers would have to do to overcome the difficulty.
If, instead of thinking of it as "difficult", we
thought of the passage as "expanding", or "climactic",
or "exploding", or even "confusing", we would be
better off. The best approach, it seems to me, is to
direct the challenge to the conscious mind, a far more
meaningful challenge than one to the physical body.
By placing our energies in the mental area, we can
begin to imagine what the sound would be like if we
were able to perform the passage as the composer
directed. The character and shape of the section then
would begin to emerge in our thinking and the achieve-
ment of these goals could then be our motivating
force, rather than the solving of a physical difficulty. As I have stated before, if you narrow your
attention you get correspondingly narrow results. And
the broadest attention will induce a positive response from the body. It will want to produce the
effect you so eagerly desire. And because you will
have given it a command which is complete in that it
includes all the qualities the music needs at that
moment, the body will be better able to react as a
whole unit. The love you have for the image of the
music in your mind will affect your own body in a
positive total way.

With this in mind, then, we might ask how one can
achieve the technique to play one's pieces. What are
the "tricks of the trade" from this point of view?
The main direction is to seek ways in which the technical "problems" can be seen as "ear" situations,
rather than "hand" situations.

18

Psychologists have demonstrated that in the human body's equipment, we are more dependent on information gathered from our eyes than from our ears. For example, it is a well known fact that the music in a movie is easily relegated to the background behind the visual action. For this reason it is sometimes a good idea to occasionally practice with one's eyes closed. One can still identify the movements of the hands on the keyboard tactilely, but without the visual stimulation the ear has more than a fighting chance to take over. Besides, I have found this occasional practice to be most inspiring from the point of view of musical creativity. One can "dream" better with the visual parts of the mind stilled.

Another way to overcome "thinking" with the hand is to play difficult passages with both hands on a single part, two octaves apart. The use of the two-octave distance, rather than just one, ensures that the work of each hand can be heard separately as well as together, thus exposing any shortcomings in one hand or the another. The question, of course, is why work with, say, the left hand on what is a right hand problem? By working with the two hands together the reflective nature of the construction of the two hands keeps the fingering from being the same for both hands, so you have a greater tendency to emphasize the sounds rather than the fingerings. In fact, the finger-oriented learner will have a baffling time of it at first to get the other hand to work correctly. In time, though, he will create a focus of attention and control which will override the physical. The sound center is the only part of the brain which can efficiently handle the problems posed by simultaneous parallel movement between the hands. He will have no other way but to use his ears to guide the fingers. Again, one must be advised to proceed slowly at first, else the passage will just be solved as a way of making the hands perform two different things at the same time, much like rubbing the belly and patting the head. No learning device can be one hundred percent effective in the face of a determined effort to undo its effectiveness.

But beyond any shortcut or device is the basic tenet that if you hear what you want to have happen, the body will do its best to achieve that result for you. As you hear ahead of where you are playing, your body is already organizing the most efficient fingering and pedalling and arm weight, etc., to give

19

you the particular configuration of sounds in your mind. This may seem difficult for some to believe, but I think a simple experiment may demonstrate that it can work. Using elementary musical materials, have a friend block off all but a single measure of music at a time, and have him move that visable measure ahead of where you are playing, always about two or three beats ahead. You will thus be forced to imagine, aurally, if you will, the measure beyond where you are playing. If you take a conservative enough pace and if you pick easy enough music for your first experiment, you will most certainly discover that the ear will tell the fingers how to organize themselves to manifest the sounds.

This is, perhaps, a rather simple experiment, and the individual can possibly find one more suited to his own situation, but I think if you approach the subject with an open mind, using materials you have not already learned, you will be able to see how the principle works. The ear can group together all the sounds of a measure or so into a coherent whole, and the hand will naturally fall into place to make the music.

Now there are times and situations where the muscular work must be done. In the beginning of one's study the hand does not "naturally" always fit the keyboard! And each finger must be made strong enough to readily accept its share of the work. Either a set of Hanon exercises will be needed, or exercises from Ernest Hutcheson's little book (Elements of Piano Technique), or some other finger and wrist strengthening work must be undertaken. Some pianists have acquired independence and strength solely through studying pieces of music, without doing exercises of any kind. If this will accomplish it, so much the better. Exercises can produce mechanical habits as well as mechanical strength, and must always be practiced with care. Nothing is worse than the "machine-gun" approach to scale passages, for instance. There are enough scale passages in the beautiful literature that we shouldn't really have to study them as an exercise. Often an unorthodox but natural scale fingering may emerge in a piece of music which produces a more fluid or more musical rendering than the one we had produced by practicing our "scales". Our unconscious should be free to suggest such innovations to us. If we are dependent in our pieces upon what we have learned in our exercises, we

20

are certainly putting the cart before the horse! Our
exercises are to give us strength and agility, not
provide the pieces of a puzzle which we then assemble
like a tinkertoy!

I will now take up, in no particular order, some
of the traditional sub-headings under the category of
"technique", and see how this approach can provide
some help in these situations.

Leaps

First, let us consider leaps. The prospect of a
rapid jump from one place on the keyboard to another
can pump fear into the heart of even the most intrepid
virtuoso. It seems this situation is so exposed, the
error so blatant when it does occur, that one sometimes feels like a novice diver about to take a certain belly-flop. Naturally, concentrating on one's
possible failure will most assuredly increase the
chances of its occurrence. Negative thoughts produce
negative actions.

Instead, we might learn something from the tightrope walker. He must think of where he is and what he
is to do next, all in a most positive manner. Likewise at the piano, we must think of where we are and
where we will be next, and not concern ourselves with
anything else. As your hand rests in the position for
playing the first note, let your mind consider the
sound that note will make. Tap it lightly to remind
yourself of its physical pitch. With your hand still
poised over the first note, think of having already
played the second note, no matter how distant it might
be from the first. Then, lightly stroke the first
note and easily position yourself to play the second.
Again, if you need to, lightly touch the second note
to reassure you of its actual sound, then give it a
nice, friendly blow. All the time your attitude must
be one of great pleasure in being so smart that you
have already completely solved this "so-called" problem! Think positively! And do not allow yourself the
luxury of a wrong note. Every attempt must be
successful in this early stage.

Soon you will discover that as you play the first
note, the second note demands to be played, and will
be played, with the precision and exactness as if you
had never even had the first note to play. Your mind
is concentrating on the two notes and not on the

21

distance between them, just as the tightrope walker is concentrating on movement forward and not on falling down or slipping off. Quickly playing two notes 23 inches apart is hard. Quickly playing two notes, each lovely in its own right, and forming together an interesting (or "bright", or "sparkling", or "startling", but never "precise", nor "correct") whole entity of sound is easy. Especially if in your fingering you do not use the extremes of the hand (1 to 5), but instead use 2 to 3, or something similar. Forget it as a "leap". Think of it as two notes, each with something to say, and let the hand move as a whole from one comfortable position to the other comfortable position.

A further variant is to play the first sound loudly and the second soft. This further reduces the emphasis on the leap and reinforces the gentleness of the movement between the two positions on the keyboard. Also it seems to help the ear to have the first of the two sounds to be connected be stronger than the second. It gives the ear more to grasp, so to speak, than the more usual upbeat to downbeat approach.

Trills

Trills are another facet of piano playing which may give us trouble from time to time. Even when we think we have mastered the art of playing two neighboring pitches in fast alternation, our fingers may let us down and one precious note fail to sound, thus breaking the continuity so important to a trill. The solution, therefore, is to try to consider this continuity, this unbroken succession of sounds, as the primary organizing factor. Again, it is important to remove our attention from the necessity of repeating the finger action as fast as possible, and place it instead on the quality of sound the trill produces. Often one can begin trilling, imagining it as endless, even to the point of being able to trill evenly and effortlessly "forever" in our minds, then with the other hand get under the arm doing the work and raise it off the keyboard. This little trick gets us out of the tightness associated with trilling "as fast as you can" between this beat and that beat.

It is important in the beginning of one's work to imagine every tone of the trill. That means singing it, and that means going slowly. It will forever remain outside one's control if it is finger action

only. Sometimes the fingers may work well, and sometimes not. Especially in longer trills, the hazard of
mind fatigue in controlling the repeated finger repetition is not just possible to occur, it is likely to.
After several seconds of giving oneself the orders to
repeat, repeat, repeat, the lifting and lowering
orders to the fingers may get a tiny bit out of syn-
chronization and a note will drop out.

The correcting concept here is to consider the
trill as forward motion. Each note is the beginning
of a little duplet. Thus, A goes to B, which goes to
A, which goes to B, etc. If there is forward movement, there is less thought of repeating notes. Instead, the quality of the movement will be focussed
upon, and, in addition, if there is any change in this
quality, emphasizing this change can help our practice. A crescendo can be exaggerated. An accellerando and/or ritardando can be introduced, if only as a
practice device. This will give the mind a particular
shape to project.

Another device which helped me understand the
nature of trills came to me as I was driving down the
freeway. I noticed that along one side the highway
department had planted a long series of bushes and
trees in alternation with one another. The shapes
complemented each other, the triangle of the little
evergreens and the spreading fullness of the little
bushes forming a solid bank of green in summer, which
was also a perfect windbreak for the snow in winter.
The bush to tree to bush to tree forcefully reminded
me of the alternating quality of trills. In fact, as
a sort of remedy for boredom I attempted to say "bush-
tree-bush-tree-bush-tree" as fast as my mind and my
mouth could manage. I found in solving such a tongue-
twister that I had to organize the sequence in such a
way that each word was the start as well as the end of
a series, hence, an endless chain. I wouldn't say
this little trick would work for everyone, but solving
the "word-trill" seemed to help me form a concept
which was useful in learning how to solve the musical
trill.

Another time in desperation I resorted to using
one finger in each hand, with the hands alternating to
produce the sound of a trill. This RH2, LH2, etc.,
absolutely took away the repeated finger action and
left me with only the sound of the trill as the organizing factor. Then, when the trill was clearly in my

mind, I went back to the regular fingering in the context of the piece, using my newly discovered sound-image to produce a smooth and continuously executed trill.

But, still, the ultimate teacher is the urgency of the music itself. I finally learned what I needed to know about trills from the end of Beethoven's Op. 111. Attention and desire must combine here in the execution of these pages of trills, where a single dropped note spells musical ruin. The thinking here must be totally positive, arising out of love and respect for the musical statement in such degree that one's "physical" technique is transcended by input from a higher source. One doesn't "ask" for help; one simply gets it. To those who have experienced this state it is no mystery. Others will have to accept the statement that it can happen, and will have to trust that when the time is right it will happen to them, too.

Tremolos

Tremolos are closely related to trills. Again, hearing each note as a "beginning" is the solving device. This seems to eliminate the fatigue-causing "down" feeling in the hand, instead causing the "up" feeling of anticipating the next note. It helps in quieter passages to use more finger motion than arm rotation, although this depends much on the size of the hand. Each will use his own equipment as he can. By keeping the originating impulse in the mind, rather than the hand or arm, fatigue can be lessened. Again, forward motion is the key. And hearing every note before you play it.

It helps to think of the two notes as "very close" to each other, even though their physical distance may be an octave. It lessens the tension if you do not have to think of how far it is between the notes, but can instead concentrate on how one note follows from the one before. This is especially easy if they are an octave apart, because the higher can be imagined as just a different version of the lower. In this case the mind can help by distorting perception as much as you want it to, when you give it the orders to do so. As in the study of trills, crescendo and diminuendo are useful practicing devices, in addition to accellerando and ritardando, as means for helping the mind to organize the motion within a shape.

24

Chords

Getting the hand to accurately form full chords is sometimes a problem for the less experienced pianist. The ear can be of assistance here. A way to help it to operate is to place the hands over the keys in question, and very lightly but precisely strike the chord, immediately placing the hands in the lap in a resting position. This last movement tends to eliminate the fatigue of maintaining the stretched out hand position. With the hands resting in the lap, attempt to hear inwardly the chord you just struck. If you cannot, repeat the process of preparing the hands over the keys, lightly striking the chord, and returning the hands to the lap. What you are aiming for is a quick placement of the hands on the keys and a light touch of the chord sound, then relaxation. Soon it will be possible to just think of the sound of the chord with the hands in the lap, and then they will in one motion leap to the chord and strike it gently and return to the lap. All this is to lead one to become confident in using the hand in "awkward" positions. Playing the chord softly helps to reduce the tight gripping with the hand, plus it promotes wrist flexibility, and it also helps confidence by reducing the physical effort required for "success".

The same principle applies when practicing chord passages where several different chords, each involving a different configuration, must be struck one after the other. Here one should place the hands carefully over the first chord position, try to imagine its sound, strike it softly, put the hands in the lap, then repeat the process with each chord in succession. Again the ultimate goal of the exercise is to be able to put the hands in the lap, imagine the sound of the first chord, lightly play it, hands in the lap, imagine the next chord, play it, and so forth, until the movement of the hands into the lap each time can gradually be eliminated. Once the confidence is instilled by being able to accurately strike the series of chords in pianissimo and with little breaks added between the chords for aural imaging, it is no trouble at all to, first, take out the breaks in time, then add the volume necessary for the passage. During this training the hand learns to relax between chords, rather than carry the tension from one chord to the next.

An adjunct to this exercise is the useful concept

of "stroking" or "scratching" the chords with an inward motion of the hand pulling towards the body. The wrist will then make a compensating upward movement, which will relax the arm. At first this movement may be contrary to the downward approach we may have been using, and will require a bit of training. It is easiest to produce when the sound is soft and short, starting with the wrist quite low. Later on, a fuller sound can be attempted, and eventually a very sharp forceful motion can be used. Octave passages are usually played in this manner by most pianists, although there may be times when a heavy downward wrist action may seem more appropriate, especially in loud volume. Sometimes it is even necessary to throw a bunch of octaves out from the shoulder, not giving much attention to the niceties of arm and wrist position if the music demands it.

Non-legato Touch

The concept of "hand-scratch" just referred to is similar to the "finger-scratch", which is most useful in non-legato passages, especially as found in the faster music of Bach. The independence of each note when produced in this manner seems to make for a harpsichord-like articulation. This is especially useful in this music because as the speed of the finger pull is increased or decreased, the resultant texture becomes either less legato or more legato. Even a single note in a phrase can be slightly more or less articulated without disturbing either the overall rhythmic flow or the basic non-legato character of the passage. And because this touch gives control over each note on an individual basis, a complex melodic structuring can be produced spontaneously on command in a performance situation, and does not have to be learned through repetition in practice.

Some have found it helpful, after having learned this light non-legato touch, to apply it to legato passages. They "think" staccato, but play legato. The impulse to each note is short and is followed by a relaxation. Not everyone will find such a concept useful, but those for whom a relaxed scale is just a wishful fantasy may want to experiment with this technique.

Arpeggios

Next I want to discuss arpeggios. These occur in

26

all shapes and sizes, and since the hands coping with them are all equally varied, there is generally no formula for success which can be universally applied by everyone. Still, the use of crescendo and diminuendo, accellerando and ritardando, is recommended to give melodic shape to the passage as a practicing device. One can't usually sing an arpeggio from one part of the keyboard to another, and because of this it is one of those figures that often gets left behind in our ear work. Yet just because of this it is most important that we slow it down and let our inner ears get ahead of our playing.

Some find the finger-scratch concept useful here, to help avoid tension which can occur as small hands expand to reach the larger chord patterns. In any case, a certain brightness of touch will help the arpeggio become more even in rhythm and thus more flowing in its movement. A strict legato is less effective in producing perceived movement through all the notes of an arpeggio than is evenness of rhythmic articulation. The ear responds more to the trigger of precisely spaced intervals of time than it does to the actualities of the connections between notes. Knowing this, it is easy to avoid the "humps" which occur as the wrist bobbles up and down to accomodate the thumb-to-fingers-to-thumb legato attempt. Once this attempt is given up, a true legato effect is produced through evenness and precision of attack. Then the whole arm provides the overall sweeping movement, so characteristic of smooth arpeggios.

Certain composers, especially Brahms and Rachmaninoff, were fond of writing left hand arpeggio passages in which the thumb was followed by the fifth finger one or two times in successive chord groupings. One little trick which helps the ear to successfully direct the hand from one position to the next is to accent the last note in each group, the note played by the thumb. That gives the ear a connecting link from the end of one hand set to the beginning of the next. Of course, this is to be dropped from the physical aspect of the sound just as soon as the passage is accurate and reliable. The mind will keep the link thus formed, however, after the artificial accents are removed.

Velocity

When it comes to the matter of velocity in gen-

27

eral, we can say that one learns how to play a passage fast by being able to hear it fast. This means going through it quite slowly, to make sure you are actually hearing every single tone. It is so easy in fast passages to train the hand to just "do" it. Then, when a mistake keeps cropping up, we are puzzled as to how to correct it. We have no access to the production of the music because our hands have "trained" themselves to overlook a certain part of the passage. When it is the mind that is able to give the orders, then the hands are trained to obey, not to do their own "thinking". So, after one has a start into the learning of a fast passage, through finger memory or hand-keyboard memory, one should back up for a day or two and secure the ear learning as well. It will pay off in security and accuracy of performance.

The same applies to those tricky ornaments and other nasty little corners in what might otherwise be an easy piece. Study these spots until singing every note feels natural, and every note comes melodically from the one before it. Then you are ready to incorporate them into the whole. Certainly one of the less agreeable sounds one can hear in a performance is the "pasted-on" ornament, which seems somehow to be squashed into an otherwise perfectly executed melody. Even the quick notes should seem to flow smoothly and effortlessly.

Generally speaking, music is not meant to sound difficult or hurried. A dramatic leap should sound dramatic. This usually means that a certain amount of extra time should be allowed for the achieving of the dramatic effect. And most often, this extra time is all we need to make the difficulty disappear. The naturalness of our arm movement is usually taken into account by the composer himself, and, in fact, a strict rendering of the notes on the mathematical beats might make us think we had to play it as if we had no human muscles at all, and were merely well greased machines. In our zeal to be competent technicians let us not forget that the composers were human, too, and they expected that their music would also sound human. Summing it all up, let us just say that technique can be a good servant, but is always a poor master.

CHAPTER FIVE

GETTING THE DETAILS RIGHT

<u>Time and Beat</u>

Rhythmic difficulties can usually be solved by involving the mind and the voice in the learning process. Trying to learn a complex pattern with the fingers is inefficient, and often may produce an unmusical result. Singing the passage in question puts the parts together in a way which is easily memorized and which relates the difficult section to the surrounding musical context.

Singing also reminds us that the basic concept in regard to rhythm is that time is what you create, not what you obey. Very often a composer will expect us to slow the pulse down to fit in a complex pattern of quick notes in a generally slow moving piece. If we solved it by the clock we would feel that the music ended up sounding rushed. Music should sound natural, and using our vocal instincts in solving rhythmic situations helps us achieve that goal.

Many pianists are troubled by the problem of "where" to put the notes of an arpeggiated chord when it appears that they should all somehow or other sound "on" the beat. Should the bottom note be struck on the beat, should the top note come on the beat, or should the beat be somewhere in between? We must realize that most of the time the chord itself <u>creates</u> the beat, so it is not really possible to answer the question the way it is formed. All the notes come "on" the beat. The "beat" in question consists of the total effect of all the notes striking.

Consider the following example. A little farm girl is returning home with her apron full of freshly picked apples, and as she runs with this load she trips and all the apples fall to the ground. One could say that they all fall "at once". And this is correct. The total sum of the individual impacts adds up to the single crash of the apples falling. Our minds easily summarize and simplify the sounds we hear to create a clearer understanding, and whether one note or another comes before or after a mathematical "beat" is not important to its perception. If it <u>sounds</u> on the beat, then it <u>is</u> on the beat.

This is certainly clear when the arpeggiated chord is fast, but what about those long drawn out chords at the ends of Chopin <u>Preludes</u> and <u>Nocturnes</u> or Brahms <u>Intermezzos</u>? They can also be solved by stretching the concept of physical time to correspond to psychologically perceived time (Ex. 1).

Ex. 1: Chopin, Prelude No. 2, in A minor

Every note in such arpeggiated chords can be considered the downbeat. Thus one may count the last two measures of the prelude: "one and two and three, three, three, three, and four and one, one, one, one, one, and two and three and four and". The "three's" and "one's" will be as close together or far apart as the music demands. In this manner, the top voice resolves rhythmically the previous melodic line by being felt as a downbeat, and the bottom voice resolves equally well the downbeat expectation of the bass line.

In the matter of appoggiatura placement a similar solution can be undertaken. Most often this comes up in a Chopin <u>Prelude</u> or <u>Nocturne</u>, and one feels in these cases that the non-chord tone should be able to give us a certain amount of its presence and then be left for the principal note. But to decide exactly how much time to give it and then to render it in a mathematically precise way would be to go against the composer's notation. If he had wanted it as a rhythmically clear melodic moment, he could and would have very well written it in ordinary notation. But instead, it is in the form of an appoggiatura (Ex. 2). So we must think of it as a vocally conceived ornament and its placement and duration will need to be determined vocally. Where is this "on the beat" likely to occur? It may easily come <u>before</u> the placement of the left hand bass note (Ex. 3). Doing so does not

Ex. 2: Chopin, Prelude No. 4, in E minor

Ex. 3: Actual sound

make the right hand sound like it is coming before the downbeat, nor does it make the left hand seem like it is coming after the downbeat. They both seem to be "on" the downbeat, and our ear generously grants to each hand its own contribution to the total downbeat effect of the passage. Because the two sounds are not struck together it simply seems more expressive, it doesn't sound wrong.

By the same logic the left hand bass note often anticipates the right hand melody in moments of heightened expressivity in romantic music. No one really cares in such situations "where" the "actual" downbeat is, because what is heard is one expressive downbeat surge, not two separate sounds. What you are doing in such situations is giving the ear information; you are not simply following directions. The difference is that giving information involves interpretation of the score and translation of it into tones. These tones are music; the score is not.

Similarly, accents in Chopin, I believe, need to be interpreted more as a vocal device than as a percussive device. As much attention to the length of the note needs to be given as is given to the increase

31

in volume (Ex. 4).

Ex. 4: Chopin, Prelude No. 4, in E minor

An accent should be perceived as an extra emphasis,
and this emphasis can in some styles more easily be
brought about by lengthening a note than by making it
louder. In such situations it is as if we stop the
forward progress of time, much like grabbing the
metronome for a moment, then we allow the normal flow
to resume. Again, it is not perceived as an intrusion
on the ordered sequence of time, but rather as a
specially emphasized moment in time.

Rubato

The whole problem of momentum and the flow of
time deserves further discussion. One is led to
expect that a beat of music will follow from the one
before by a predictable amount of time. What makes
this unit of time, or beat, predictable is not always
just its regularity. A rising phrase needs more time
at the climax, as a diminishing phrase needs more time
as it dissolves. Sometimes an expansion and compres-
sion of time can occur within one hand, while the
other maintains a steady even flow of pulses. This is
the "rubato" referred to by Mozart and Chopin in their
letters (as possible in such passages as Ex. 5 and 6).
The singer is already perfectly acquainted with this
phenomenon, as he "toys" with the placement of his
melodic line above a regularly spaced accompaniment.
The best singers never sing expressive music precisely
on the beat, but find a perfect balance between free-
dom and discretion in the flexibility of their melodic
pulse.

The other kind of rubato is more common in piano
music. In this the expressive needs of the music
cause the entire texture, both right and left hands,
to slow down or accelerate. Usually this is easily
felt and executed, much as in a pleasant walk through

Ex. 5: Mozart, Sonata, K.311, in D

Ex. 6: Chopin, Ballade No. 4, in F minor

the woods we slow down to admire a pretty flower along
our path. Our pace may slacken for a moment, but the
direction and intent of our motion is never impaired.
For some the image of putting the brakes on while the
engine is still pressuring us forward is a good image.
The feeling of momentum and its forward motion must
never be lost, or we will flounder in the uncertainty
and incomprehensibility of the passage of time. Time
must always be expressive.

Even in its most regularly predictable form, as
in a march or dance tempo, the music expresses the joy
we feel as our body participates vicariously in the
physical expression of the dance. The difference
between a mathematical rendition and an uplifting,
though equally precise, rendition is apparent at once
to the discerning listener. This differnce is usually
manifested through the quality of the "up" beats. In
sensitively performed dance movements the upbeats im-
part tremendous vitality through their slight emphasis
(Ex. 7). The music seems to want to go forward be-

Ex. 7: Bach, Gavotte, from French Suite in E

cause the downbeats themselves are not accented. Instead, the energy is sent forward from the upbeat to
the downbeat, and to the next upbeat again. One need
look no further than the other music of Bach to see
how supremely conscious this great composer was of the
power of offbeat phrasing. Because of this quality of
momentum we find it usually necessary to close a movement of Bach with a strong ritard. This slowing down
is required to disperse the accumulated momentum, and
usually the longer the piece, the greater the ritard
needed. One doesn't feel this need to ritard in the
faster movements of Mozart or Beethoven because the
energy is already dissipated sufficiently through the
use of contrasting material within the movement.

Polyrhythms

     Music in which the performer is asked to play
different rhythms simultaneously can create problems.
In fact, for the pianist who is learning his music
primarily in his fingers, these polyrhythms often are
one of the hardest parts of a new piece. Because this
is essentially a mind problem, new working methods may
have to be developed by these pianists.

     Every polyrhythmic situation must be approached
in three ways: what one hand does, what the other
does, and what they do together. Generally speaking,
if sufficient attention is given to learning by ear
what each hand does, it is not as difficult as one
might think to conceive of how they will sound together. It is absolutely essential to relate the
activity of each hand to the flow of the downbeats.
Thus, in a Chopin passage of seven notes in the right
hand over three in the left (Ex. 8), it is far easier
to memorize the sound and feel of what the seven are

Ex. 8: Chopin, Waltz in A minor

doing as they move from one downbeat to the next, unrelated to the activity of the left hand triplet, than to try to solve the two together mathematically. When the necessary rubato is included at the beginning of one's study of such a place, the performer is thinking melodically from the start. In fact, many can solve such oddly related time configurations at sight because their aural imagery can accomodate the melody and the accompaniment as two separate, but coexisting, elements. What ties it together are the downbeats in both hands coinciding.

However, there are times when things are not so easy, and the combination just cannot be imagined in the ear at sight. And for some even the pattern of three over two, or two over three, is impossible to conceive of. In these situations it may be necessary to construct a graphic model, so that the eye can assist the mind in grasping the combination. One can draw a line on a piece of paper and put marks on the top side of the line representing, say, the right hand triplets, at zero, two, four, and six inches (Ex. 9).

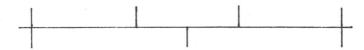

Ex. 9: 3 in RH over 2 in LH

Then on the bottom edge of the line put marks at zero, three, and six inches to represent the left hand duple rhythm. Even the earliest beginner should have no trouble converting the spatial image to a sound image. Slapping the thighs with each hand separately and then together usually is a good preparatory exercise.

Solving four against three can be done using this

method also, although some may prefer to write out the
note values of the combination sound as a single line
of rhythms, showing by notation of the stems whether
it is the right or left hand which plays at any moment
(Ex. 10).

Ex. 10: 4 in RH over 3 in LH

However, in the more complicated patterns found in
contemporary music, such as ten against seven, or four
against five, the method of using the diagram is fail-
safe. After the strange new combination is practiced
and eventually absorbed into the mind, the ear is able
to keep this image as it separates the music of each
hand from the total.

Work with both hands slapping the thighs first,
then with one hand on the keyboard and one on the
thigh, then reverse the hand positions, and finally
try both on the keyboard. It can be done! It will
probably help to try to learn the faster moving voice
first and then fit the slower one into the faster. The
mind seems to find that method easier, and memorization is also quicker. Still, eventually you will need
to have the two sounds as a single sound in your mind,
as well as the separate sounds each moving independently of the other. Whether you conceive the combination sound first or the separate sounds first will
depend on you and on the music, but there should come
a time when both ways of listening are simultaneously
possible.

One should not forget that in some composers, no-
tably Bach, Chopin, and Brahms, the notation of six
over two is often a polyrhythm. The six, when studied
alone, may more easily be understood as three groups
of two, rather than two groups of three. Should this
be the case, one will need to practice the six by itself, hearing it as a divided triplet within its melodic context, then add the slower moving part against
it. Many of Chopin's "fioratura" ornaments, when
approached in this manner, are likewise seen as con-
taining a metrical structure independent of the left
hand accompaniment (Ex. 11). Conceiving of them in
this way helps to project their "flight" above the

36

Ex. 11: Chopin, Nocturne, Op. 9, No. 3, in B

otherwise restrictive left hand figure.

There is another way of learning polyrhythmic
figures and though it is not at all mathematical, it
should not be overlooked. For instance, at the end of
Chopin's Nocturne in D-flat, there are groups of
seven over an accompaniment grouped in six (Ex. 12).

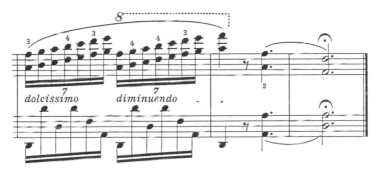

Ex. 12: Chopin, Nocturne in D-flat

The solution is easy: all you have to do is play the
right hand a tiny bit faster than the left, and after
a few tries you will find exactly the correct increase
to allow time for one extra note. The same method can
be used for five over six. Just slow the top hand
down until the rate is reached which brings the five
into alignment with the six. It sounds difficult or
even impossible if you have never done anything like
it before, but some find it the best, or at least the
quickest, way to solve many polyrhythms. Thus, seven
over three can be solved by first playing only six
over three, then speeding up to allow for the seventh
note. Again, the passage will need to be practiced

until the voices can be heard both as being two sep-
ate things together, and as being a single complex
thing.

Metronome Marks

Metronome marks are sometimes a source of confu-
sion to the novice, even when the composer himself has
added them. One would think that a number is a number
is a number, and one should just follow the metronome
mark and that should be that. But when the metronome
mark goes against all of our previous experience, or
is so fast that it is unattainable, we wonder what to
do. It would be simple to say that the composer must
have added it in a moment of exuberance and that the
fast tempo should not be taken literally. But we cannot lightly accuse composers of being sloppy, and we
owe it to them to search out a better explanation.
Many have said that the speed of something inside
one's head can be quite easily half again as fast as
the sound one might want in a real performance. This,
plus the light touch on older pianos, seems sufficient
to excuse some over-fast marks in Beethoven. But the
Chopin Nocturnes are the real puzzle. I certainly
don't have "the answer", but it has helped me to consider his marks to be the "ideal" tempo, if there were
nothing in the music which would cause us to slow
down. But in the Nocturnes there is almost always
something beautiful and expressive happening, so we
are almost always slowing down from our "basic tempo".

Tempo

Chopin's use of the word "lento" deserves some
caution. The "slow" to which he refers is most often
the larger unit in a compound meter. Look at the
Nocturnes (Ex. 13, 14).

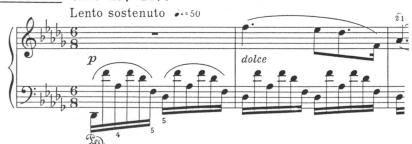

Ex. 13: Chopin, Nocturne in D-flat

38

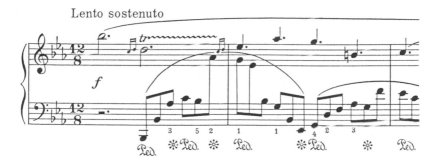

Lento sostenuto

Ex. 14: Chopin, Nocturne, Op. 55, No. 2, in E-flat

If the eighth-note in six-eight meter is taken as the
basic pulse, then "lento" would be slow indeed. Similarly, I suppose that is why the "Moonlight" Sonata of
Beethoven is taken so slowly. People neglect to see
the "alla breve". The tempo mark refers to the large
pulse, not the small pulse. And in a waltz, "lento"
refers to the whole measure moving slowly, not each
beat. A minuet is in three, but a waltz is in one.
They just look the same. No one from the early 1800's
would have ever mixed up the two. Our being at a remove historically can sometimes put us at a disadvan-
tage. In the same way, a "presto" in the classical
period is "quick", but in the baroque period is only
"lively". A good music dictionary can help straighten
out these points.

Fingering

Now I would like to take up the subject of fingering. Or, rather, I would <u>not</u> like to take it up.
I will try to explain. In my own study I started out
as many do, deciding the very best fingering to use
and pencilling it in over the notes. In polyphonic
music this even meant carefully notating every time a
finger changed on a note. I was thorough. Then, as I
discovered the joys of sight reading, and the ability
to play whole handfuls of notes without the slightest
attention to fingering, I began to notate my fingering
in my more seriously practiced pieces more and more
lightly. If I didn't have a problem I would not
notate it at all.

Whether I notated it or not, however, at this
stage I stuck to one fingering, unless I decided I had
figured out a better one, then I changed it. But

because I was learning my music at this time from the finger movements, there was always the possibility that in a tight spot during a performance I might revert back to the old fingering, or, worse yet, might not be able to play the passage at all, because a conflict might have been set up between the old and the new fingerings.

All this was resolved one day when I decided I would really just let the fingering find its own way. By this time I had discovered learning by ear, and the pleasure I got from carefree sight reading I took over into my performance repertoire. I was determined to let the body truly seek the sound in its own way, and leave the muscular coordination to the unconscious. And I still do this 99% of the time now. There are only a very few places where my unconscious isn't quite up to the task, when the music gets too complicated, and I must consciously decide what finger to use.

My hands do still learn the fingering automatically. No one is immune from this. But the hands are free to choose another fingering in performance, should a whim of musical expression occur to me which I had never considered before. And a friend once told me a story how, after taking a finger-stinging blow from hitting the top of the fallboard with his finger by accident in a particularly furious passage, he needed to make an adjustment of an altogether different nature. He had hurt his right hand fourth finger and just ahead lay the end of the Chopin <u>Preludes</u> and a five-octave descending passage, where the fourth finger would be asked to come crashing down on a B-flat six times in quick succession (Ex. 15).

Ex. 15: Chopin, Prelude No. 24, in D minor

He decided he simply couldn't do it; his finger still hurt too much, so instead he split the passage alternately between the hands, an octave for each hand, thus avoiding the fourth finger, and got every note, even though he had not ever practiced that way. Others have told me of similar situations. We can be flexible when we are using our ears as guides, and letting our fingers follow naturally the instructions we give them. Their "learned behavior", though unconscious, remains amenable to conscious control and can be changed or altered as the situation demands.

Another time when this lesson was driven home for me was when I learned a suite by Henry Purcell and decided it would be more authentic if I improvised all the ornamentation, since in his music the ornaments are all notated, but it is not stated specifically which type of ornament is preferred. I religiously prohibited myself from playing the piece the same way each time, and instead relied on the inspiration of the moment to guide me in the selection and execution of the ornaments, of which there were a great number, often several in a single measure. This experience was a very healthful one for me, because it showed me that I could improvise during a performance, and it proved to me that I could play whatever I thought of, even though I had not practiced it. I think we could all use such a lesson now and then. We get so tied down to habits that we forget that the whole point of performance is to re-create, not demonstrate.

Phrasing

Phrasing is an area which is often taught one way to beginners and in another way to more advanced students. As beginners we are taught to lift the hand at the end of a phrase, and that is supposed to be that. But more advanced performers discover that a phrase mark is just a way of showing the pianist that the notes within it are to be played as belonging together, and to delineate one phrase from another there are many more means available than just lifting the hand. One can slow down to show the end of a phrase, one can accent the beginning of a phrase, one can shape the phrase with dynamics, and in all these methods one never needs to interrupt the legato flow by lifting the hand between phrases.

If it would be helpful, you might want to examine Chopin's Prelude in F-sharp Minor, where the whole shape of the piece is made clear through the length of the phrases, yet there is no place where one would

41

want to stop the flow by lifting the hand (Ex. 16).

Ex. 16: Chopin, Prelude No. 8, in F-sharp minor

Some mistakenly think that where no phrasing is indicated they are supposed to use a non-legato touch for the passage. This may possibly be, but it may also be that "no phrasing" means "no grouping", and the best touch might be a tight legato. One should just remember that phrased music should be structured into parts, which are somehow made clear to the ear, and unphrased music means that the sound is unstructured and continuous. The rest is up to the performer to decide.

It is here that the importance of the edition should again be stressed. So many editors have felt that the notes were the composer's creation, but the phrasing was the editor's responsibility. That makes about as much sense as deciding to correct a poet's grammar or punctuation. No composer writing after 1780 was careless in his phrasing, and it is sometimes absolutely disruptive to the musical structure and thought to tamper with what the composer wrote. Most scholarly editions are especially careful on this point and are to be commended. The times seem to have changed and no longer are we inundated with numerous "false" editions. Those who are using older editions would do well to compare them with a good modern urtext to see to what extent there have been unannounced changes in phrasing, as well as in dynamics and pedalling, to mention only a couple of the possible areas of transformation.

Pedalling

Pedalling itself is sometimes of great concern to a composer, but sometimes it is hardly notated at all. Probably the best thing to do is to notice carefully how the composer has used the pedal marks, and then decide for yourself how to interpret them. Older pianos were less resonant than our present instruments, but, still, some of those long pedals in Beethoven and Chopin are delicious (Ex. 17, 18, 19)!

Ex. 17: Beethoven, Sonata, Op. 53, in C

Ex. 18: Beethoven, Sonata, Op. 31, No. 2, in D minor

43

Ex. 19: Chopin, Prelude No. 6, in B minor

We must try playing more softly to see if we can approximate the effect they wanted. Fluttering the pedal or using "half-pedal" technique are also to be recommended as possible substitutes for the long pedal. But sometimes there is no recourse other than just holding that right foot down and let come what may. Not all the surprising sounds you will get are going to be disagreeable or unintelligible. And sometimes it is murkiness that they actually wanted, or they would never have written the long pedals in the first place.

Chopin's pedals in particular deserve special attention. His manuscript facsimiles show us how fanatical he was in regard to just exactly where the pedal was to be depressed and where released. His scratchings-out and corrections are evidence of his continued attempt to improve the final version before it was sent to the printer. But there are many places where there is no pedal indication at all. Are we to play these passages without pedal, or is their treatment to be left to our own discretion? There is no way to really know, but my answer has been to give it a go without pedal and see what happens. Usually the conclusion is that the pedalling was too obvious to write down, or it was too complicated to be able to be written down. But occasionally there are places where a dry passage is just right to contrast, say, with a pedalled passage coming up next (Ex. 20). Obviously the choice is the performer's, but the main point is that there is a choice, and that we do not have to prejudice ourselves to one or another course of action without first trying the passage out in several ways and then evaluating them in terms of what they produce.

What do we do in the case of Bach and other early

44

Ex. 20: Chopin, Ballade in G minor

composers whose music was written for the harpsichord?
Perhaps the best answer is to play their music exclu-
sively on the harpsichord! But for most this is not
possible, and for some not even desirable, so we find
pianists usually in one of two schools. The first say
that a piano should sound like a piano, and they use
all possible pianistic techniques, including both the
sustaining and the una corda pedals, to achieve whatever variety of sound they find appropriate. Others
say that the piano is indeed a flexible instrument and
can by judicious use of non-legato technique approximate the texture of the harpsichord. For these the
pedals are taboo, since they did not exist on the
harpsichord. Variety of sound is limited to what the
harpsichord could produce, that is, variety of articulation and registration. But this leaves out the
tremendous variation in timbre between treble and bass
in the harpsichord, and it leaves out its utter clar-
ity in enunciating the separate lines of a polyphonic
texture, so some kind of compromise, it seems to me,
is advised. Obviously, it will be up to the performer
himself to decide how best to show the baroque style
on the piano. My own solution, for whatever it is
worth, is to avoid pedal, generally using a non-legato
or at least a less legato touch in the active music,

45

and using variety in the dynamics to show the individual lines in polyphonic music and to show the phrase structure in the dances.

There are places where the fingers can help the feet. Those gifted with large hands are able to hold down the bass note in an accompaniment figure, and not put the pedal down right away. They can hold the bass note and keep the previous pedal sound longer than just barely into the new measure. Then when they change pedal their little finger is on the note they need as the bottom of the next sustained sound. Some places sound really wonderful with this kind of overlap. Of course, those with small hands will not be able to develop this technique, unless they are able to stretch their hands to resemble those of Chopin, which were not large, but had extraordinary stretching capability. Some of the longer added note values in the upper parts of Chopin's _Nocturne_ accompaniments seem possible only with a hand that could stretch a large tenth. In addition, Chopin wrote unbroken chords of this size, and so it is very possible that he used this "finger-pedalling" technique, since he had the means.

There are a couple of situations in which we can be advised to not use the pedal, even where our normal expectation would be that one might be required. One is when we are rushing downward towards the bottom of the keyboard in some vigorous passage. The movement of the line as we reach the last octave or so of the piano is made clearer if we leave the last several notes unpedalled. The ear can then follow the line all the way to the bottom.

Another place to consider omitting the pedal is in a pianissimo passage. Sometimes we just can't get the piano we are using soft enough, or sometimes a change of color is needed, and the thinness of soft, dry, una corda sounds is just what we need. It is especially useful just before a heavily pedalled lyrical section, when the transitional passage might be also slightly ritarded as well as left unpedalled.

All this advice about how to realize the details of the piano score is meant to be just that--advice. It is meant to open doors, not close them. No person can tell another how to be an artist, and should he try to do so, he will be defeating his purpose even if he feels he is succeeding. One can be guided by a

46

teacher or colleague, but ultimately every decision must be his own. You just have to remember that when you are performing there is only one person in charge --yourself.

CHAPTER SIX

A POSITIVE APPROACH TO TEACHING

The whole point of piano lessons is for the teacher to train the student to teach himself. And in order for this to be accomplished, the student needs to be able to draw upon the higher centers of the mind in a consistent and successful way. The piano lesson should foster this way of thinking at all times.

You can get the student to learn more by asking him questions than you can by any other way. It gets him to form connective links in his mind. Putting the links there yourself is not the same. You need to supply the situation which in itself is a kind of question, and then he is motivated to seek the answer himself. Then, when he finds the answer it is his, not yours. He will see things differently than you, even such basic things as "why make music?" The answers we have found to this and other questions work well for ourselves, but cannot possibly work equally well for everyone else.

I have found, for instance, that it is of great benefit to let the student perform his first piece of the lesson in its entirety before making any comments. After all, one of the things you are trying to teach the student is how to perform, so it makes sense to give him a try at making a good performance. By not interrupting him you allow him to produce something which he can think of as a whole thing. If you stop him, or make him "try it again" after a minor breakdown, he begins to do it for you rather than for himself. His attitude then becomes one of trying to please you rather than trying to create something of value in its own right.

This is certainly a fine line. It is true that you must urge him on to bigger and better things, but if you give him an impossible goal, he gets frustrated and discouraged. There should always be that element of loving everything he does, even the most disordered, uneven performance. If he has put out an effort, he should be commended for the effort. At the same time the results can be evaluated quite objectively. Probably this can be summed up by saying that you love him because he is a good person, but you need evidence to prove whether he is a good pianist or not. That way you help him to do his best, but keep your musical judgment as objective as possible.

There _are_ times, though, when you just want to push him right off the piano bench, sit down yourself, and just plain show him how to do it! These moments of exasperation will actually be appreciated by him, and he will be glad you broke out of your emotional reserve to prove to him how it could be done. But most of the time he will more readily respond to your suggestions if they are given in the spirit of helping him discover for himself what to do at the piano. He has to know that your respect and warmth of feeling for him go on truly no matter what he does. This trust is probably the most important aspect of the teaching situation.

After the student has learned to hold things together well on the small scale of, say, pieces of two or three pages in length, and is ready for something more challenging, you might consider giving him something sectional in nature rather than continuous. By this I mean a set of variations or a fantasy, rather than a sonata movement. First of all, in a sectional piece there are several types of technical work required, and usually the same type of technique persists over a few lines, so he is given a full opportunity to master it, not just a measure or two. Second, he needs to learn how to build long shapes, and training him to accumulate sections together to produce a whole is easier than trying to help him to construct a complex, highly ordered sonata movement. After sectional pieces (which also might include the minuet and trio) good stepping stones toward mastering the presentation of the first movement of a sonata would be the slow movement, or the last movement, both of which are usually more clearly divided as to formal structure than the first movement. This is only a rough plan, obviously, since every piece of music has its own particular character and challenge, but if you are attempting to help the student master the art of presenting whole things, then the repertoire studied should be approached according to how it fits in with such a purpose.

In sectional works, for example, it is possible for the student to build a conscious plan of the way the character of the piece changes. First it might be "placid", then awakening by degrees, such as "restless", to "energetic", to "sparkling". The good teacher will have dozens, or perhaps hundreds, of

such character words at his command. They are so useful that if you feel the need it might be worth the
effort to consult a good thesaurus or dictionary of
synonyms in order to compile several lists of similar
but slightly differing descriptive adjectives from
which to choose.
    So often I have asked the younger student, "How
should this sound?", or "What is the character of this
section?" Most often they have not yet acquired the
necessary vocabulary to convert their feelings into
words. Or, often they actually need a stimulus from
the teacher before they get the idea that all these
notes could produce a single concept, and one of
these "miracle" words, such as "crystalline" or
"somber" might be all they need. When they appear
completely tongue-tied I have found it useful to ask
them if it should be, say, "brassy", or "grandiose",
or "fierce", just to give them the chance to decide
for themselves, and this returns the music-making
decisions back to them. It is easy, sometimes, to
forget that they are young, and have not had much
experience in trying to explain things verbally.
Getting your thoughts across to another person is
clearly a wonderful way to increase your vocabulary.
I can say for myself that until I began teaching I
didn't know very many of these special descriptive
character words.

    Sometimes expressions such as "clownlike", "like
an elephant dance", or "like the wind talking", can
stimulate the student to exaggerate the qualities of
the music. Most inexperienced performers need to
learn about projection. In their daily life they are
taught to frown on imaginative exaggeration, so when
they discover they are in a situation where the free
use of the imagination is encouraged and is necessary
to help the projection of the music, they might need
assistance and encouragement in indulging their fan-
tasies.

    The use of character words can even be applied to
a single chord. The voicing (relative loudness of
each tone in the chord) may vary as words such as
"deep", "resonant", "thundering" or the like are used.
The training of the hands to distribute the sounds
within a chord in particular ways is made easier by
considering the effect of the whole, rather than by
training the fingers to respond individually to accept
a greater or lesser proportion of the arm weight. The
teacher can demonstrate the sound as the student calls

51

out the verbal commands of one character or another. This can be quite a revealing and rewarding experience, as he hears immediately how a single two-handed chord can be made to sound any number of different ways, just by thinking differently about the effect it is supposed to produce.

Often in the course of a pianist's study the path from ear to hands is reversed. The fingers go along playing a piece over and over again until the way the fingers move begins to condition how the ear "thinks". We play a passage in a certain, perhaps erroneous, way, and when we try to gain control with our ear, we discover that the ear has already decided how the music should sound and is locked into dependency upon input from the muscles for its conceptualization. This is certainly a dangerous state and will need to be dealt with forcefully. When a student seems to be having this trouble it is best to have him play the right hand part with the left hand. Or, the technique I mentioned previously of playing the difficult passage with both hands on the same part, but separated by two octaves, will also help to retrieve it. As I mentioned before in discussing technique, there are times when attention must of necessity be focussed on the physical mechanism. One must simply train the muscles in a new type of movement, or away from a counter-productive type of movement. Often we inherit another teacher's failings when we accept a student with previous training. Bad habits are bad habits, and will need to be broken with some force. But a little while after the new way of successfully working has settled in, the ear will be able to take over, because it will have less resistance to overcome. I still consider that such situations should be given every chance to be solved without recourse to lowering the consciousness to the muscular level, but I admit that if the ear has been blocked off there is nothing else for it but to re-educate the hands.

If you will use as your basic premise that there is no such thing as a teaching problem, that there are just situations that need to be understood, then your teaching can remain positive. Of course, this is just semantics, but in approaching something that may appear to be a problem, we need to remind ourselves of all the "problems" in our own work that we have solved by simply believing we could solve them. Or the necessity of circumstances or schedule or whatever made us have to solve them. Necessity is the mother of invention, and positiveness is her ally.

For instance, some things seem easier to do when they are not done by ear, say, sight reading, and this might seem like a problem for the teacher. Many students see the relations between the notes and translate these visual cues directly into muscular action. Of course, the mind has to work a little when sharps and flats are present, but this is able to be learned through location rather than by sound. Nevertheless, I still recommend learning how to sight read by ear, because the ear can order the approaching sounds with more musicality than the hands, and after a little practice, with more fluency and better hand coordination.

There are several techniques to help a student engage the ear in sight reading. The first is one I mentioned previously. Block off from the score all but the measure after the one he has just played. At first let him stop and study that measure until he can hear it well, every note, then have him play it up to tempo. Repeat this process with the next measure, and so on. Eventually what you are working for is for him to be able to play and continuously look ahead and hear what he is about to play, but it takes a bit of practice to get to this point, even with easy music.

Another technique is to study an eight-bar section away from the piano. Then, when the student can hear both hands easily in his mind he will be ready to play it. It is best to seek a tempo which will allow a fluent, accurate performance. Sometimes this means a pretty slow tempo, but, depending on the music, it might even be possible to play it the first time by ear and up to tempo.

One authority advises playing along with the student an octave or two above him, using specially chosen materials in which each hand maintains its position within an octave. I have tried this, and it works pretty well, and I would add that playing along an octave below the left hand is also helpful in its turn. Ensemble of every sort is a useful aid to sight reading. The motivation factor is high. You force yourself to look ahead because one or more people are counting on you. The ear is called upon in this situation because often you are looking at not just your own part, but at the other parts as well. Most of the best sight readers I know say they learned how to do it through ensemble playing, and <u>all</u> the best sight readers I know say they hear what they are about to play before they play it.

An extreme case occurred when a friend came to visit me one day and volunteered to accompany a Beethoven concerto I was preparing. When I heard the fantastic sounds emerge from his piano I was shocked. I had studied the orchestral "reduction" and found it next to impossible to read, much less to play. He said he wasn't actually playing what he saw. Instead, he heard in his head the sounds he saw on the page, then he simplified that into something his hands were able to play. He reduced the "reduction"! And all instantly, and all by ear!

Singing one part while playing the other works well as a prelude to reading both together. When asked to do this the student invariably picks the right hand part to sing, but do not let him neglect the left! It is certainly far from easy to sing the left and play the right, but it gets the ear involved in the area where it is least likely to go on its own.

"Sight reading" is perhaps a misleading term. What we are attempting to do is help the student acquire the skill of being able to see music and play music at the same time, using the ear imagery as the go-between. This can be practiced with music one has never seen before, or equally effectively with more familiar music. So "reading" is probably a better term for what we are aiming for. To do so at sight is nice and is a very useful tool, but the practice sessions may continue to use sight-reading materials even after they become somewhat learned. When they are learned to the point where the student is no longer reading them, they should be put aside.

Singing is useful in many other ways. After all, if you can sing something it proves you can hear it first. There are some shy types that have trained themselves to be unable to sing except with others. Often they will be able to sing along with the teacher, and eventually some can learn to sing alone. For those for whom any kind of vocalization is too scarey or too difficult I suggest whistling or even playing a kazoo. Often their inhibitions are able to be by-passed by having them produce their tones through such a musical instrument. It somehow exposes them less because of its tonal distortion.

54

I think everyone is familiar with the virtues of singing in regard to the study of polyphonic music, but to many this practice is confined to singing along while playing each part in turn. One can also, say, in a four-part fugue, sing each part in turn while leaving that part out in the hands, playing only the other three. This actually helps the student to play the other three by ear also, because of the changes in the fingering which will naturally occur. Playing all four parts, emphasizing the volume of only one throughout is also a good technique, whether one sings along with the emphasized part or not. Playing only one part and singing another, especially when the two are near each other in range, is good because it overrides the fingering habits, and also isolates the voices from the whole for clearer hearing.

Getting two students to play and sing a two-part invention or dance movement is a social event as well as a learning situation. When the boy sings the lower part in the correct range, and the girl sings her part, each playing the other's part on the keyboard, the result is spectacular. After this a terrific performance can be produced by having them leave out the singing but continue to play. They will be so used to hearing the other part from having to sing it that it will be an exhilarating experience to be able to play only one part but truly hear both.

In all kinds of two-piano or four-hand ensemble situations it is advised to get students to practice both parts. I have often assigned that both parts be learned by both players, knowing full well in my mind who was eventually destined to play which part, but not letting them know my "decision" until well into rehearsals. Doing it this way ensures that they will hear the whole musical texture, not just their own part.

Whether the teacher has two pianos or not in his studio, it is possible for him to play along with the student, either substituting for one of the student's hands, or doubling above or below the student. A teacher can, through an ensemble situation, help the student understand something that words cannot always easily convey. A picture may be worth a thousand words, but in the piano lesson the teacher's participation through ensemble may be worth a million!

The tape recorder might be worth another million.

Through its use in the lesson the student can hear himself objectively. It is valuable not only because it exposes mistakes, but it also gives the student the thrill of hearing his own excellent playing, even though it might include an occasional lapse from the ideal. Somehow it is more believable when it comes from the machine, probably because it is physical sound only, not sound plus mentally imagined sound. I have heard students exclaim with surprise, "Hey, I sound pretty good!" No amount of praise from the teacher can exceed the value to the student of his own positive critical response.

But it is a most valuable tool in isolating an error for close scrutiny. Reel-to-reels can be played at half speed for further dissection of difficulties. This is especially useful for inaccuracies in rhythm and in ornamentation. The reel-to-reel recorder can also double the tempo, which occasionally comes in handy when you want a metronome beat faster than is possible on your machine. Sometimes it is good to put a metronome beat on every sixteenth note to help the student get away from accenting groups of notes. Just record, for example, at 180 beats per minute, double the reel speed and you get a metronome at 360. Since being able to play fast by ear means having to learn first how to think of the sounds quickly, this technique can be a helpful one.

Some teachers have a good quality cassette recorder in their studios. The virtue of using cassettes is that the student himself can easily purchase an inexpensive machine for his own use. There are endless possibilities. The teacher could record the solution to a complex rhythmic situation; or the student could bring in his best performance of the week; or the student could even listen to his whole lesson again if he wanted to. The student could become the teacher at home by recording the performance of a piece, then he could give himself a critique of it. The ensemble partner could record his part for the other pianist's practice sessions. The list goes on and on.

By far the most important reward from using a tape recorder is that it puts the student in a performing situation. Once the "record" button has been pressed it is as if he is in the recording studio and the little red light has come on. He knows that he is going to hear himself afterwards, so he exercises his concentration to make sure he has something later he will be proud of. I have found, in my own work, that after a while it didn't matter whether I actually took the trouble to play the tape back. I was instantly transformed into a performer the second I saw the tape turning.

Thus the "performer's consciousness" can begin to emerge, either at home or in the teacher's studio. Some teachers wait to use the recorder during the lesson until the proper time, then they say, "All right, now, let's do that piece for the recorder." This gives the student a chance to be a little nervous and he will try harder. Some students even make a collection on a separate tape of their best performances, to be dubbed onto other tapes later for friends as Christmas gifts. Having such a collection is good for the student's morale, also, because it enables him to hear how much progress he has made over the months or years.

Every lesson ought to include some performance. One of my teachers was quite clever in this regard. He would always delay the end of the lesson until the next student had arrived. Then he would ask that I play my piece again for the next student. Having this "second chance" at a performance, after having already played the piece once for the teacher, gave me quite a boost and was crucial in helping me develop a positive attitude toward performing.

If at all possible every teacher ought to have a weekly performance class. I find that two hours set aside on a Saturday morning for a free added session enhances the value of the private lesson experience in countless ways. The students get to meet one another, for one thing. Often they come from opposite parts of town and each is the only person in his peer group seriously interested in the arts. To meet and talk with others who share their excitement about music is a valuable part of their educational experience.

Student performances are not the only thing that can go on in these sessions. The instructor can get to perform, too! And it doesn't hurt to have the students, or the instructor, perform the same piece each week for several weeks. After all, how can one improve something if one doesn't practice it? It also helps the students to have the teacher share in the performances because it shows him as being just as

57

human as anyone else. It tends to make the group feel that they are all sharing the experience of learning, rather than being divided into two classes of people, the knowing and the unknowing.

Tape recordings of the performance class can be made for subsequent playback during the student's lesson. Often this moment is the highlight of the lesson because the student can hear himself doing his best work, and in addition his self-criticism is much more objective because he is able to view his performance from some distance.

In the performance class another thing that is fun is to play several commercial recordings of the same work and discuss their virtues and shortcomings. A sense of what is appropriate for the different stylistic periods can begin to be developed here. And when the occasion presents itself, a discussion of a public performance attended by the group the previous week can further help the students form standards of sound criticism. In addition, a visit to a museum, or a play, or a dance recital, might expand their youthful world. We shouldn't forget that quite often they rely on us for most, if not all, of their artistic education, and it is up to us to accept that challenge happily and with enthusiasm.

The performance class might be a good place to teach improvisation, too. By this I mean free improvisation, not merely learning to add a left hand to a given melody. A composer lurks inside every musician. It is part of the package, so to speak, and we need to encourage its expression by providing an immediate outlet for this type of creative energy. Sometimes joint improvisation on two pianos, where one person feeds inspiration to the other, is even better than solo work. I personally am an advocate of public improvisation, and conclude every concert of my own with an extemporaneous piece that I "compose" on the spot. Some will say it is impossible for them to do such a thing, and that may be so, but one is far more likely to succeed as an improviser if one has had encouragement as a student in the art, and has had a forum in which to practice it.

Everything that one intends to do well needs a good beginning. And it is possible from the very first piano lesson to teach the principles we have been discussing, that of approaching things as wholes, and that of learning music by ear. It is quite easy, for example, to get the beginning student to be aware of the importance of an evenly flowing series of beats by having him consider his little eight-bar piece as a whole thing. "I couldn't understand it," becomes a much more meaningful comment than, "That beat came in late." When you tell him that you couldn't understand it, he may ask you why. Even if he doesn't and you have to explain what you meant, it is more healthful for his attitude to be trying to give you something you can understand than to be trying to do a "good job" for you. He will have enough of that in any case. The first, more adult, attitude is harder to develop, and when you can structure things so as to encourage its function you are doing him a great service.

If the hesitation persists, then have him come to a complete stop at that place and add enough time to solve the difficulty. Understanding that there was a difficulty is the first thing to impress upon his awareness. Adding time to get his mind in a new "set" can work wonders. The added time can be gradually withdrawn in each run-through until he feels confident to try it with no delay at all. Then you can say, "Now I really understand it!"

Generally the principle involved is to make the student aware of his error, then add a moment for conscious thought and change of habit, then gradually through repeated practice, withdraw the added time element. In the case of a wrong note the same applies. Get him so he can come to the spot and stop, then consciously be able to choose either the right note or the wrong one, upon your command. Then he will have control over it. Just learning the right note isn't always enough. He has to consciously un-learn the wrong one, too.

You must help the student develop honesty in his practicing. Often he may want to play a piece so much that he does not face the fact that he is messing it up. His body will then proceed to efficiently learn all the wrong notes and rhythmic distortions just as thoroughly as if he had learned the piece correctly. That is why the tape recorder is so good, even at the beginning of one's study. Or, I should say, especially at the beginning, because he gets to train himself to listen critically to his playing early in the game.

As I have previously mentioned, slow practice is the path to playing by ear. But how slow? Slow enough for there to be no errors, for one thing. Students are often amazed at how slow this must be. "Slow is slow," I often find myself saying. We all need to put our expectations out in front of us to examine. When we expect more than we are able to produce, here again we just end up practicing our mistakes. Also, slow practice should always have some kind of musicality to it. Concepts such as "slow motion", "instant replay", or the like, are more meaningful than "slow down", because they include the idea of forward motion. If you are still going forward in your practice, you have included the momentum of the passage in question. Tone and texture and shape are hard to maintain in slow work, but momentum is not.

The development of the ear can be further expanded by the use of a music fundamentals book, especially one that uses records, like Tom Manoff's Music Kit. In this approach the elements of rhythm, pitch, and timbre are learned by participating vocally and physically with recordings as well as through written exercises. Books like this are usually almost self-teaching, so valuable time need not be taken from the lesson going over endless drills. In addition, many school and even pre-school programs these days emphasize the acquisition of basic musical skills, much to the benefit of the piano teacher as well as to the student.

At some time during the lessons it may be useful to have a "practice" practice. Just have the student pretend you are not there and let him show you what he does at home. Naturally, he will show you his best work, and it will challenge him during the week to remember how hard he was able to work for you during the lesson. It takes up "valuable" time, but it shows us truly what kind of work the student is doing at home, and it provides us with a good opportunity to demonstrate to him in detail whatever aspect of the learning process he may be neglecting.

One last word on another way of getting the ears to control the fingers. It is certainly a "make-believe" method--it is only in the student's mind--but it works. In slow practice have the student form an association of the "sound about to happen" with the "skin of his fingertips" about to play. That is, as he plays have him imagine the sound as being "con-

60

tained" in the fingertip skin at that moment. Artificial, of course, but the association will persist, and soon he will feel the fingers and the sound to be one, and that is what you want.

It is important that we help the student to use his higher centers by challenging him to think for himself, rather than having him become proficient at taking orders. Learning should always be in terms of self-discovery. The moment we say, "Stop asking questions. Just do it," we have changed the experience from one of finding out about something to just "being a good boy". Piano lessons should be an unpredictable, exciting growth experience. Everything possible should be done to stimulate the musical, intellectual, and creative forces within the student. It is the teacher's responsibility always to remember this.

CHAPTER SEVEN

SUCCESSFUL PERFORMANCE

Ask a pianist why he performs and you will get a variety of answers: "Because I like the way it makes me feel," or, "Because I like to show off what I can do," or, "Because the music needs someone to get it out," or, "Because my teacher says I have to!"

Many students start off with one of the first three answers, but after a while they end up with the last. They just get too nervous for it to be the pleasure they thought it ought to be. Now, if they don't know their music, or if they have it locked away in the unconscious and are out of touch with it, then they should be nervous, because disaster can and probably will strike without warning. But knowing one's music isn't the whole cure for nervousness. We can practice correctly and still become so distracted by the performance situation that we are unable to play well.

There are quite a number of things that can disrupt our thought patterns. Just thinking about being up there in front of all those people is one. Worry about making a mess of the notes is another. Also, I remember in my early days having quite a time accepting the fact that I was responsible to all those people for their musical enjoyment. I didn't think I was worth their attention. Being a "star" was about the last thing I wanted to be.

If we think about it a minute we will see that the role of the actor and the role of the pianist are not far apart. Both "learn their lines" and, after sufficient rehearsal, present their art to the public. But what is different is the nature of the rehearsal. The actor, first of all, is involved with other actors, with scenery, with props, and with a familiar stage. He has other actors and the director for his "audience" at every run-through, and usually a guest or two in addition to help him get used to their reactions. By the time the show opens he has complete confidence in himself and has even accustomed himself to where the laughs will come. He knows how the props will feel and he knows how the room will sound.

Contrast that with the poor piano student! Often the best he can manage is a run-through on the stage piano, and in a joint recital he has to contend with other equally ill-prepared colleagues backstage. And most important, the actor is used to being looked at, is used to being the "star", while the pianist is completely surprised by the sensation. Of course, this is not always the case, because the very best teachers always prepare their students well for recitals, but too often it happens that the teacher is too busy to supervise all the details, or that we are our own teacher and need help in organizing our own preparation.

Probably the first level of preparation, then, is to find a fellow aspirant and use each other as a "practice audience". Also, I have my students bring a friend to the lesson to be the "listener" when they are preparing for a performance. And as I have described before, the use of the tape recorder can help, plus the studio performance class exists as a major training ground. But when recital time comes closer we need to approximate the actual situation in more detail. We need strangers in the audience. We need two or more rehearsals in the performance hall, the last one being a "full dress rehearsal" in "full costume" and with as many in the audience as we can get to come. Then when D-day arrives we will be ready.

But what do we do when we have done all that and we still find ourselves in the middle of the first piece thinking, "Oh, oh. My mind isn't thinking of the music, but my hands are still playing! Oh, help!" We can still be distracted no matter how thorough our preparation. After all, we are human! The thing to do is to immediately begin singing the music inside your head. That will, first of all, give you something to concentrate on other than whatever distracted you, and if you have learned your pieces by ear it will give your muscles the particular stimuli they are used to having, and you will be able to continue the performance without interruption.

It is actually possible to practice this "getting back" procedure. After all, the most distracting element in a performance is ourselves. We discover, much to our surprise, that we are playing the piano! We study our fingers as if seeing them for the first time. So, as a practice technique we need to find something that will call our attention to ourselves in a way which might be similar to what happens during a performance. I have found that it works really well,

64

first, to start performing your piece for someone and, after getting into it a ways, then, in a loud and clear voice, announce your name, first and last, to the world. Saying our name aloud like that tends to embarrass us a bit, and that is quite similar to the self-conscious feeling we have on the stage. After we say our name we should begin to think, "Get back! Sing your piece!", all the while not letting a single note drop out. Other distracting situations: have a friend scratch the wall, shuffle his feet, wrinkle cellophane, etc., etc. Always have him wait between times until you are well back into your piece before he does "his thing" again.

In my own performance I do not consider a piece mature enough to be ready to play in public until I have performed it for friends three different times. The first time is to prove to myself I can play it, the second is when I begin to enjoy playing it and begin to feel the inspiration which I know has to be there, and the third is so that I know I can count on the inspiration to be there every time. Only then do I dare to bring a piece out into the world. After all, at the end of a performance it's not too nice to have to stand up and tell the audience that you apologize for the shaky performance because it was the first time out with that piece! All your performances should sound ready and relaxed. You owe it to your audience to give them nothing but your very best every time.

There is another psychological situation that comes up often. Students seem more afraid when they play for their peers than they are when they play at a jury examination where the audience consists solely of teachers. I think they figure that teachers are used to hearing mistakes, so it really doesn't make it much different from a lesson. Not so with their friends. They especially want to play it perfectly for their friends. Making a mistake or having a memory slip seems about the worst sort of event they can imagine. The trouble is that they are consciously asking themselves to perform "perfectly", but, knowing inside that they are human and that perfection can't really exist, they "project" the demand for perfection onto the audience. In their minds it is the audience that expects them to do it perfectly, whereas in real life their loving friends would be the first to excuse an error.

This analysis may not be accurate for every case of "perfectionitis", but talking about it from this point of view with a student (or with oneself) may bring out the true situation, whatever it might be. When they realize they are creating a false expectation within themselves, there is a good chance they will relax and accept what comes. And, naturally, after such an insight what comes is a beautiful, flowing performance.

The importance of not trying to "do a perfect one", but instead "make a good one" cannot be brought out too strongly. Mistakes will happen. When they are forgotten as soon as they occur, the remainder of the performance can still be intact, but when the first little mistake becomes a disaster of major importance and destroys the composure of the performer, then the effect of the music as a whole suffers. It is almost as if when you play from the point of view of an improviser you are "beyond mistakes". The moment is all that counts. And when that moment is filled with love for the music, rather than worry about what might go wrong, at least you have a fighting chance of making something worthwhile.

There are occasions where the piano is in such poor shape or so badly out of tune that the sounds you are making may bear very little resemblance to the piece you rehearsed. This is especially a problem when the sounds are complex and dissonant. I will never forget the time I graciously offered to perform the Alban Berg <u>Sonata</u> in the home of a local music club lady, and when I tried out the piano realized it was not really too badly out of tune with itself, but the whole keyboard was about a quarter-tone flat overall. Now, I don't have perfect pitch, but I have something like it in that when I sit down to play my pieces I hear them in the proper key. Just sitting down in front of the keyboard seems to trigger my memory bank and the correct sounds come to mind. Well, I managed to somehow brazen it out. After all, it was I who had asked to play, because I needed the performance experience, so I would have been too embarrassed to ask to be excused. And what I found was that, although I did know the piece by ear, my original learning had been by memorizing the hand positions and movements, and when the ear couldn't really help, I was lucky enough to still have those early associations at my command. My advice to myself after that experience, and hence my advice to you, is that

66

if you decide to play something dissonant and atonal be sure to continue to actively rehearse the hand positions even after you have learned the piece by ear. You won't regret it!

Another thing I have noticed is that I may have a slip or a mistake in a passage immediately after a difficult section. I think what is happening here is that I say to myself, "Well, I got that part pretty well, didn't I?" And in the precise moment I am thinking those words I am not properly attending to the passage I am actually playing. The hands are going through the motions, but I am not directing them properly with the ear. So, in a performance I find that those parts, the parts right after the hard parts, have not been learned correctly and will sometimes break down.

And for those who are afraid that when they walk out to the piano, acknowledge the applause, sit down, adjust the bench, and are ready to play, they will forget what comes next, I have the following advice: use the name of the piece as the "cue" for the first note. Just practice sitting down, announcing the piece in your mind, and playing the first phrase or two. Like any other conditioned response, this one will always work if practiced sufficiently.

So many pianists arrange their programs to follow the chronological ordering of their pieces, and often end up beginning with Bach. For many this means big trouble. The mind needs all the composure it can muster to handle polyphonic music, and at the beginning of your performance you might still be a bit tight, if not downright jumpy! Starting with something slow and comfortable might be advised until one gets more experienced and can manage his program solely from the point of view of the aesthetic effect it will produce. It won't do you any good to have a brilliantly conceived program if, every time you play it, you bumble through the first ten minutes until you can settle down and finally be yourself.

Some inexperienced performers can't seem to handle the applause. It throws off their concentration because they are so conditioned to thinking of the pieces and being in their own world that it comes as a shock to be made so forcefully aware of the audience. Part of the rehearsal technique should, therefore, include forceful applause from the "audience". And it

67

ought to include bows, too. When the fledgling performer realizes that all a bow is is a ritualized
acceptance of the "thank-you" of the public, then it
will just seem a fair exchange: you applaud; I bow.
No amount of rigid, tin-soldier-type action is called
for. A simple, relaxed motion of the body, expressing
one's natural humbleness, is all that is required.

I guess everyone develops their own routine for
what to do on the day they are to perform. It does
seem to be the general consensus, however, to avoid
performing your pieces "at full tilt" the same day you
are to play them in public. It uses up all your reac-
tive energy and none is left for the evening. For a
performance to be vital the performer needs to react
to his own playing, and having already done so earlier
in the day means that the piece will sound "old hat"
and less interesting the second time. Your desire to
play the piece is the motivating force for what will
hold it together in your mind. If you have already
performed it that day, there cannot be the same eager-
ness later.

The general consensus is also that one should
always go through as much of the program as possible
the same day, but should hold back the actual performance involvement. This usually means less dynamic
contrast, less speed, and less energy in general.
This procedure seems to work well. You remind yourself of the finger and hand movements necessary to
play the piece, and your ear also has a chance at its
work one more time.

If this can be done early in the day, all the
better. The afternoon needs to be allowed usually for
the piano to be tuned and for the performer to rest.
A walk in the woods and an hour's nap are to be recommended. Last-minute practicing produces last-minute
nerves. We don't need it.

When I was touring, and playing four or five con-
certs a week, I followed a definite order of priority.
First in importance was sleep. I would give up all to
get my required number of hours in bed. Next was
rest. During the day I found periods when I would do
nothing much at all. Third was proper diet. This
meant eating carefully chosen food well in advance of
the concert, with supper around four or five o'clock
in the afternoon. And fourth, in its proper place,
came practice. If it appeared that the other three

had to be slighted in order to find time for practicing, I would instead curtail the practicing. I
found I could play a lot better when I had rested than
when I had crammed in some practice.

All this advice is not to be taken, however, if
you honestly think you are not properly prepared to
play your pieces. In the beginning of my touring I
was still very insecure in both memory and execution
and practiced four or five hours a day, trying to get
through everything very carefully, mending and patch-
ing as necessary to be able to somehow get through the
program that evening. I don't recommend being as un-
prepared as I was, but if that's the way it is, then
you'd better practice up to the very minute you go on
stage!

I have also found that talking to my audience
helps my performance. At first I thought that talking would only distract me from thinking of the music,
and I had better stay away from it. But I found that
talking helps the public to relax, and a relaxed audience is more attentive, which helps me concentrate
more easily. And what do I talk about? About myself,
mostly, before I start the program, then later I give
them something specifically informative before each
group on the program. I don't try to tell them "what
to listen for". I believe this does more harm than
good, because it narrows their attention rather then
opening it up. They are so busy concentrating on what
they are "supposed to hear" that they fail to use
completely their sensitivity to music. This limits
their reaction to the mental level, and thus closes
them off to higher areas of appreciation.

Instead, I try to give them information in a general way about the type of piece I am about to play.
I translate foreign words in the titles. And I try to
be light and humorous. This helps them overcome the
prejudice that so many inexperienced listeners have
that classical music is "stuffy" and "pretentious",
and not of much interest to ordinary people. I think
they appreciate my efforts to reach them on their
level, and I certainly appreciate their increased
attentiveness. Afterwards I often hear something
like, "I'm so glad you talked to us. It made you seem
so much more human." I wonder how many of us forget
how "inhuman" we must appear up there, in tails, or in
a formal gown, doing something so far removed from the
area of the audience's normal experience that it must

be impossible for them to see us in their own terms. If we are honestly trying to share something with them, rather than dazzle them with our technique or feats of memory, we might give a little more thought as to the manner of our presentation, so that we don't intimidate them from becoming personally involved in the artistic experience. After all, in the final analysis it _is_ the listener who the composer is attempting to reach through the performance.

Talent is free, but gift must be earned. Many can get up in front of an audience and play beautifully, but the _inspired_ performance always leaves us breathless. How do we receive this divine gift? We cannot ask for it, but, instead, must earn it with our love of the music. We empty ouselves of our ego, our selfish point of view, and through dedication to the beauty which has been left to us by generations of composers, we learn discipline and self-realization. When you are thus opened up, the higher forces can find in you a proper vehicle through which to present to the world the uplifting benefits of great music.

This whole philosophy has been expressed well by Hermann Hesse in his novel _Siddharta_, in which he has his character say: "When someone is seeking it happens quite easily that he only sees the thing he is seeking; that he is unable to find anything, unable to absorb anything, because he is thinking only of the thing he is seeking, because he has a goal, because he is obsessed with his goal. Seeking means: to have a goal; but finding means: to be receptive, to have no goal."

Or, to put it more simply: when you reach the point that you can stop asking questions, then you will begin to get the answers.